AMBER SHONETTE BURWELL

Foreword By:

Pastor Jeffrey Whittaker

A Glimpse of Her Story Vol. II

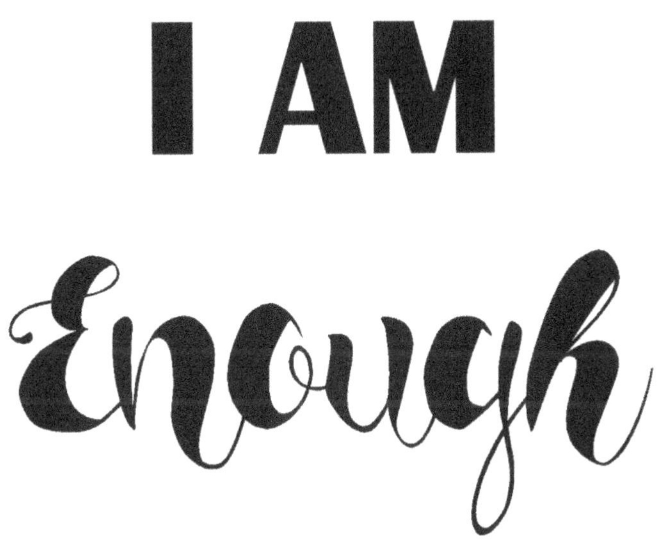

AMBER SHONETTE BURWELL

 Unless otherwise noted. Scripture references are taken from the King James Version of the Bible.

ISBN: 978-0-578-85201-0

Cover Design: Danielle Ludy, Ludy Media Group
Instagram: @deludy26
Facebook: @Danielle Simmons-Ludy

Interior Design: Danielle Ludy, Ludy Media Group

Photography and Makeup: Miracle Etheridge
Instagram: @miracletransformations_

Printed in the United States of America

Praises for I AM Enough

Food for your soul is what comes to mind when I think of "I Am Enough". Amber walks through the intimate parts of the journey that is needed to gain a footing in purpose. It is pivotal that we know who we are in Christ and just as pivotal to know the assignment for our lives. In these pages Amber unmasked the truth of the struggles that entangle us while we struggle to properly navigate our emotions of past pains, what we believe to be as failures and the torment of our own personal timelines that we have set in place and attempt to obligate God to fulfill those objectives. The fear of not being enough is a giant that we all at some points have faced, to hear the steps of endurance from an overcomer not only inspires but propels us forward. Great Read!

Kiyanni Bryan *@kiyannib*
Author. Speaker. Coach - Consultant. Publisher
Kiyanni Impacts LLC / Write It Out Publishing LLC.

This book is going to change the trajectory of so many lives. I've been in such a STUCK place; this is exactly what I needed to start the process of healing and moving forward. There are so many gems it's almost unbelievable. To anyone reading this devotional, this is the beginning to such a beautiful story. We are more than enough!!!

Amber Lloyd
CEO/Founder @shopashestoamber

Dear Beautiful soul, within the scribbled lines of text of this book, you will find the ever reaching, merciful, and grace filled words of God. You will be soothed, stitched, corrected and made whole in the broken areas of your soul. It's clear from the opening paragraph that the author is not merely sharing life experience. She has gone far and beyond that, positioning herself in heavens prescribed posture of yielding everything to be used by the Father. Dear beautiful soul, I encourage you to soak in the presence of the Lord that resides in every piece of this text and to savor the sweet moments that the Lord takes to speak directly to you. We will never be the same and I thank God for it.

Andre Mason
Entrepreneur
CEO/Founder @amasonapparel

Dedication:

- *Mommy, here are your flowers, your answered prayers. I love you so much.*

- *To my grandsons Major Chance and Chosen Sincere.*

- *To my granddaughter Legacy Katourè*

- *To the memory of my grandchild that was lost on 01/28/2020.*

- *To the life, memory and legacy of my God mother Apostle Norvice G. Sellers.*

- *To every soul that needs the reminder of just how beautiful you are, here it is...*

I AM ENOUGH

Foreword

The moment we become resolved with who we are, in the eyes of God, is the moment we become free to fulfill the purpose for which we were born. As you navigate through the pages of this book, Amber spiritually, transparently and practically expresses the journey to her discovery of self in God. Using a combination of Biblical truths and personal experiences, Amber teaches us how to embrace the person God saw in the womb. In Psalm 139:13-14 the psalmist David writes, "You made all the delicate, inner parts of my body and knit me together in my mother's womb. Thank you for making me so wonderfully complex! Your workmanship is marvelous—how well I know it." David shows us, in the last five words of this psalm, the most important part of one's purpose: knowing it.

The knowledge we have of ourselves governs the way in which we live our lives. This could be beneficial or burdensome depending on what we have learned and accepted as truth. Too often we allow our experiences, and what we've gained from them, to determine our identity. We let hurt, disappointments, failures and past decisions define who we are. Deceptively, these experiences lead to the entrapment of our truest potential, and as a consequence, hinder the intentions of God for our life.

It's not until the eyes of our heart are opened to the truth of our self-worth, the inward value revealed to us by the Spirit of God that we begin to see we are more than enough. We come to understand, the value of our life is not determined by our decisions. No, the significance of our existence rest in the discovery of who we are to God. What you are about to read is the process of someone whose revelation of this truth was made known. From pain to promise, Amber Burwell shares her story so that you'll be able to embrace your own and realize you too are enough.

Jeffrey Whittaker (@letsgrowjeff)
Lead Campus Pastor
All Nations Worship Assembly-VA

Preface

It's hard to believe that almost seven years have passed since I released my first book, "**A Glimpse of Her Story",** on April 8, 2014. After the release I had come up with every topic, title and vision for my next project but more so, I let the lies of the enemy, fear of doing it again and procrastination set in. So much has happened in these nearly seven years. Yet still, I remain humble and grateful for the opportunity to not only be transparent but also transformed in my mind and life through the *process*.

After the release of volume one I was naïve enough to think that I was done healing from one of the hardest phases and seasons of my life.... **WRONG**!!! Of course, it wasn't just divorce but the entire discovery I made *within* the confines of my divorce that needed healing were also waiting and they finally had names: ***depression***, ***lust***, ***uncertainty***, ***insecurity*** and ***fear*** among a much longer list of stuff. Volume one was huge for me but in the midst of these nearly seven years heightened self-discovery has been much bigger. Allow me to go back for a minute:

November 19th, 2016, I heard God say something to me and almost chalked it up to just hearing something and therefore almost brushed it off and missed the revelation behind it. The word was ***RENOVATION***. With that I saw an entire construction team ready to come in and do some work. That morning, I was finally committed to the gym, so I was headed there also. I sensed that day demands from my future and my destiny one of which was to begin rising early, seeking the Father desperately *BUT* to be ready and competent to handle all that God wanted to do and ultimately require from me.

Renovation was starting in my mind and in my temple and I also needed to accept that God needed me to obey Him regardless of the cost and inconvenience personally. Honestly, I was tired of committing to new processes, I just wanted to be DONE and basking in the promise also known as the lazy and easy way out. That day, clarity came and that was my Father was then and still is "*making me*". During the renovation process which lasted one year God wanted to show me what He could salvage but also wanted me to trust His plan for what we resolved together about what couldn't be fixed. In that, God showed me that He could still provide some type of remedy even for that too. I can write it is one of God's gifts to me, but I also want to be sensitive to His voice and to the needs of His people. I want my private life to match my public display and I want to love like He commands me to and how He already loves me. I certainly didn't want to rush my next book for the sake of a self-imposed deadline and damage someone and/or myself but I wanted to make sure I have either mastered or am submitted to what I am writing about. I am now.

In January of 2018, my Pastor gave me a prophetic word and that was that I would enter the things God placed in me from a "*pure place*" as I had been meditating on the next book God shared with me purity is not just about purity in body, or a movement or what I don't indulge in, but true purity is having "**a pure heart**". Ultimately the way I (and others) *see God* through me.

A major part of my second book is behind me and that is the direction. I am BACK! It is my prayer to be more effective and extremely transparent then I would have been immediately after the first installation. Today my journey and the journey for those that will hold this book in their hands begins yet again. When one journey ends you don't just stop because most likely there is another one right behind that one, one more tedious, one longer and one to teach and show you more. It's a part of life.

Life does indeed happen to us all, things come at us that shake and rock us at our core, we wonder if we will ever recover and ever get back to the things that matter and mean something to us. We wonder if we can ever evict the thoughts that plague us, the pain that numbs us and if the storms will ever cease from raging.

We wonder if it's worth it. If the past that calls and pulls on us daily is safer than the future that is challenging us to be a better, updated and a more refined model of our selves. In all of this (hopefully) we discover our soul anchored in Christ and our stance unmovable. There will always be a test we will have to pass and a new level that awaits us once we do. I will say it again: life will happen and happen to us all but if you can see greater beyond your now you are ready, really ready, to go beyond and to embrace heaven on earth.

You my friend are ready to embrace "*life after*" and you're ready to enter the place you only imagined and dreamed of. A huge part in arriving at this place is "***acceptance***" of where you've come from, where you are right now and where you're headed. Acceptance shouldn't be mistaken for agreement, they're not synonymous. Acceptance, however, is to resolve the internal war that is produced when we look to reconcile ourselves to our current moment.

In other words, we want the Lord to help us make some sense of it, to help us see and to know without a doubt He was there all along.
I have had during this journey a huge issue with my timeline vs. the timing of God. I think honestly it has been an issue for me most of my life and due to severe frustration and being deceived during these seven years especially, my timeline has tried to haunt and trap me. Ultimately, it's what's kept me away from doing this again as well (publishing). I have had to really pray through and pray against anxiety and comparison. I have had to learn how to commend myself for a job well done and even for a job almost done. I have had many ideas that I have drug my feet on because I was waiting on backing and/or to be affirmed by certain individuals. Wait! If I didn't get affirmed then I felt the need to make sure they saw, or they knew that "*it was me*" that did it! Yup that was me.

At the center of all of this? You guessed it! rejection and even abandonment. One of the roots that inspired this book and have caused me to peel back so many layers. It took me great time and courage to write volume one and I poured so much of myself into it but as I sit and type it's evident that God is requiring so much more of me (and you as well). He desires for people to get delivered, find hope and safety in you (and I) "**telling our story**". It is important that you define what that means personally, after you solidify how to go about doing that and once you've nailed that down get busy. Do it now, don't wait!

While you wait the people that need hope in your voice and even from what you've been through also wait and what a tragedy it is to withhold someone's next and even their strength (that your story would give them) in your possession. That statement isn't to add pressure to your already full plate it's just to show the value of the treasure in your (earthen) vessel our heavenly Father has placed in you and on you.

To all my family and my friends thank you for rocking with me, if you haven't done so, get caught up on who I am from volume one because we are going deeper this go round all for the Glory of God and all for those attached to me.

C'mon and go with me! My name is Amber, and I would like to welcome you to "A Glimpse of Her Story" Vol. II.

Introduction

I am ready for you to receive my pour, my transparency and to hear my heart on this topic. This is fresh to me but necessary to share. I remember the entire process of my first book and how the seven months that it took me to write it didn't feel like much in comparison to all that I shared. One thing I remember sharing is how my entire life I have always felt either out of place or vastly different. In the time since penning volume one it's come to life for me even more.

Unfortunately, I have journeyed with people and even found myself in circumstances since volume one that I compromised a lot especially who I know I am at my core just to be accepted to be rescued and to receive relief and reprieve. I have questioned on various occasions purpose and the huge demand and standard that God has placed on my life. Sometimes to be quite honest it does not seem fair.

In 2019 I was given the opportunity to share my writing monthly via blogging with, **The Wholeness Pursuit**. My blog topic: "Inner

Healing", which is a passion of mine to dig deep and to help others dig deeper also. With this this opportunity came exposure of my writing to a new audience all while learning and still developing as well. While doing so I discovered through this platform how important inner healing is and that I was still in the process of healing. I also discovered how therapeutic writing is for me. It literally has snatched me back from making a wrong turn at the crossroad of my life.

Writing has also forced me to mastery and making sure I am truly ready for the dimension, depth and level God has shown me for my life and the life of others that I touch. I can say a part of me has struggled with unbelief and insecurity with my successes and those that I have helped to share their stories. Through each people encounter God has shown me that this is what I was born to do. In this, I have realized those that are called to me, and I am assigned to, we will not miss each other and no matter how many opportunities present themselves the true and authentic ones will be what stand and stick.
I did not plan to go in this direction for this book so I stand in awe of all that Holy Spirit will do thorough my hands. This will be a project for

anyone that has ever questioned your identity and felt that it was tied to a specific person or group of individuals or even an event. It's not! Sure, a solid team is good, necessary even and those you can trust too but at the end of the day it is not mandatory to *start* doing the work and chipping away at your purpose.

The word **enough** in simple terms means: "*as much or as many as required*". When I say and I boldly declare "**I am enough**" it comes from a place of right now as I stand, and right now as I am. Sure! we always want to leave room for evolving, for improving and for coming into full fruition and knowledge of who God made us to be and His view of us. If all of the aforementioned took place years from now, today, at the current time, and in your current state "***you are enough***". That is what Volume two is called **I AM ENOUGH.** Selah!

On January 31st (2020) the Lord stopped my current direction and told me to reroute. I am enough is about coming face to face with true identity and letting go of what doesn't and who doesn't belong in your life while recovering quickly who and what's supposed to be. This is a book that will force you to dig to find your why all while severing anything insignificant from the past. This is a precious and fragile moment and should be handled with care. I am going to be brutally honest not just throughout but even now when I say I don't have the full direction of what this will mean when we reach the end, but I do have a heart to obey God and to watch this unfold. Are you ready? I mean really ready to not just explore being enough but to feel the fullness of what it means to your life to carry out all that is required of you because you know you're enough? How does that sound? I know. Just imagine walking in true freedom and liberty from the opinions and the desire to be accepted by others. Now that you've imagined it lets journey to it. Let's go just grab what you have.

I am reminded of the scripture that says to whom much is given, much is required (Luke 12:48). I know it's been hard and great amounts of pressure thus far with being you and being called to change the world. But I want you to also anticipate who's being made in this, who is being molded and perfected. Those persons deserve just as much attention as who you used to be gets. Rest assured God makes no mistakes not even when He

chose you to lead, when He chose you as His called.
Let's go! We are getting ready to dive in fully, we are getting ready to immerse ourselves in territories and paths unknown but are so very critical and crucial for us. We are getting ready to let out a sigh of relief for language on where we've been all while experiencing something new. We are getting ready to find ourselves strengthened like we didn't know possible and in a realm that we could have only imagined. It's here, we're here, and I sense something amazing on the horizon. Come on let's go we have work to do.

I AM ENOUGH!

A word from the author....

Still Forward!

"Look up the sun is ahead and it's time to move forward." These the words that ended chapter thirteen of volume one. I was done, I was ready to actually get moving. While I did in fact move, I also got winded, fatigued and wondered at times if I was moving at all (maybe I was on a treadmill or something) but all in all I had to somehow keep it moving. Why? Well, I answered this in chapter fourteen of volume one when I said, "greatness is never behind you, it's always before you."

Before I dive into the content for this Volume I, want to let you know that the posture and the motion is "***still forward***". It'll always be that. So, you may want to draw it out on poster board or something. It's important to make this known because there is always the temptation to revert backward, to chill, to take a break and even bask in your wins. While basking is okay make sure you're **still** moving. Make sure you're still accessing and make sure your heart is clear and free (this is super important).

Since volume one I realized that forward didn't mean much or what I thought it did because there was partially a fleshly connotation attached to it for me. Forward while letting "them" know, (a whole other book). Now I am grasping forward in all that I do and even in who I am the right way. I want you to do the same.

So, limping…we will still move forward. Frustrated, forward. Depressed, forward. Uncertain, forward. You catch my drift? Good, because no matter what, how or what you must sacrifice you're going forward!

You are enough and you are competent. Among many reasons one of the clearest is because of your choice to move forward. You have to know that this is the only direction and stance for you. Ever.

So, when you're faced with what seems insurmountable or something that feels too heavy, make a directional choice first and that would be that you're going to move now and every step thereafter forward.

We ended the last book and now we begin letting all who we will encounter know that we are moving forward and we're going anywhere but backwards. This decree feels good, doesn't it?

Section 1: THIRST

"What we want is not more little books about Christianity, but more little books by Christians on other subjects—with their Christianity latent."

~ C. S. Lewis

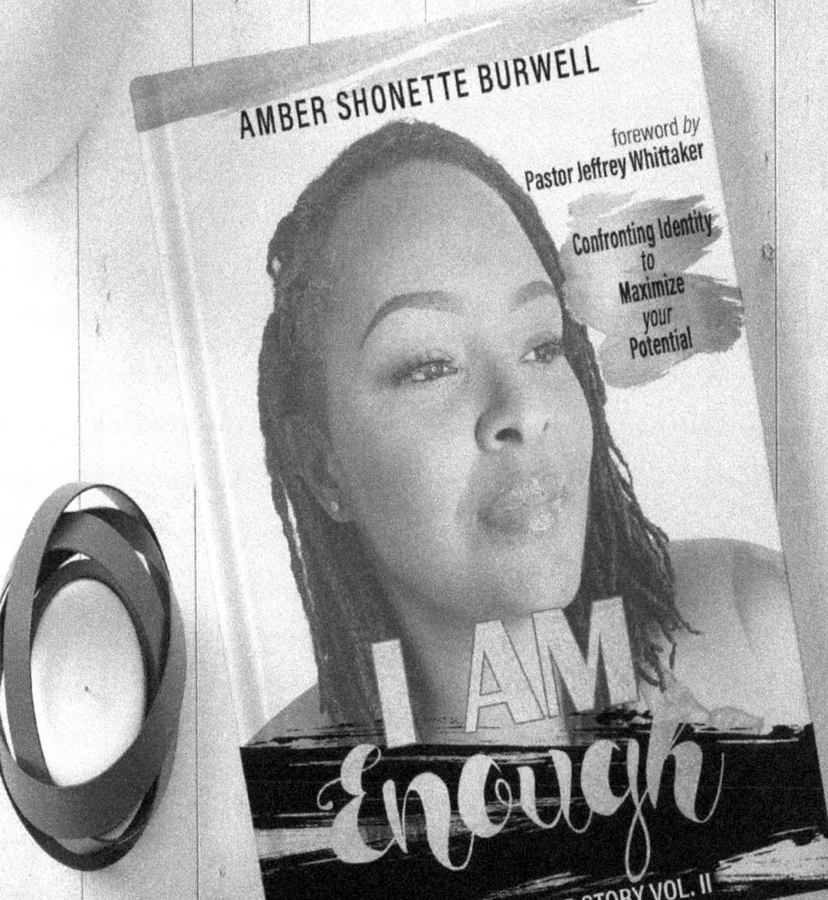

AMBER SHONETTE BURWELL
foreword by
Pastor Jeffrey Whittaker
Confronting Identity
to
Maximize
your
Potential
I AM
Enough
STORY VOL. II

DISCIPLESHIP

Show me someone who is running on fumes, double minded, being taken out by every storm sent their way and I assure you at the core is a lack of discipline. I wish I could tell you that discipline would be something you'll need every now and again for where you're headed or that you won't need a lot of it when you get to where you're headed. Not the case! In order to be promoted to the level of promise you've seen it is going to take a level of discipline that you have never committed to. You may have top notch discipline already and for that I commend you but in order to go even higher you won't be able to survive off of even that.

All of what God shows you isn't for you, there are others attached to your promise as well as your obedience and this is one of the reasons why in all things, we have to become disciplined. Our destiny demands our discipline. In the end you'll begin to experience the breath and the favor of God on all you do.

Discipline is what causes your momentum not to fizzle out and die after it has been built. Discipline is the habits that are built and sustained today for the moments and the life that you will have tomorrow. Discipline is a necessary not often spoken of entity that we all need. Discipline doesn't feel good, and discipline requires a great level of sacrifice. This level of sacrifice is for what is to come.

Your training ground for your destiny is your lifestyle of discipline which causes our lives to yield righteous fruit. It causes our lives to yield blessings because of our obedience to God. Discipline is necessary for where you're headed. You will not be able to live a life void of discipline and expect to last and expect to prosper.

How do you start? You start with the things you do daily, you start with how your day begins. If you know you're easily distracted and the things you indulge in don't bring you closer to your expected end, end them now. Discipline is non transferrable. Every level and dimension you reach

God will require a new level and dimension of discipline that accompanies where He is taking you.
I pray now that we receive fresh discipline and that we allow our diet(s) both naturally and spiritually to be disciplined as well. May you be kept and guided to be sustained, have a greater awareness of the discipline we lack and need to be successful.

May we rise early, may we keep going when no one is looking and may we not overextend our "cheat" (relax) days. May we see discipline as necessary to all that we're called to do, and may we not let temporary fix and/or pleasure stand in the way of discipline's reward.

A huge and major part of our identity is wrapped up in our discipline. Before you're empowered with more you have to master your now in the form of leading a disciplined life and a balanced life. Move some things around and change some things too you are enough, and you're disciplined too.

Today I will: Dig deeper!

- [ ] My current disciplines.

- [ ] My future disciplines.

- [ ] Why?

- [ ] Who you're destined to be depends on it.

In the end:

You Are Enough!

Dear Beautiful Soul:

Thank you for taking the time to read this letter, this journal entry if you will and what will get your own mind going and wheels turning. At the core of my call and my assignment has been an intense lack of discipline. I've wanted things handed to me, I wanted the trauma in my story to repay me huge dividends and can be honest? Neither have happened. So, if you identify with any of this, I admonish you to not be like me. Your destiny can't outlive your lack of discipline.

The times I felt like not enough and I really focused on it at the root was having too much time to focus on it. LOL sounds simple right? It is but what I am really saying and admitting to is a disciplined vessel isn't questioning or considering their value and one of the reasons is there's no time to do so and no person that can make them do so or convince them anything contrary to who they are.
You're enough already. Yes you! Your adaptation of this truth will be found in your discipline.
Ready. Set. Go!

Get started on bringing order and structure to your days and your life in the form of discipline. You beautiful soul are enough!

Dear Abba:

IDENTIFICATION

In your declaration of being enough and in your dig and your pursuit of the things God has for you and is doing inside of you there are a few things you must be settled on: who you are in Christ and the authority He has given you in the earth. Identification in the spirit realm can be very sensitive because we live in an age where our credentials, titles and accomplishments are what we use to describe who we are and ultimately as our validation of who we are.

When we introduce ourselves, we may start with the family line we come from, who we may know in common with someone or what we do well. Have you ever heard someone introduce themselves by their failures? I haven't either. Don't get me wrong what I have described above is a part of who we are but it's not the sum of who we are. It's a small piece to a much bigger picture. I have found in my life that just because I can do a thing well it doesn't mean that I am truly connected with it or that it really is a part of me. You can do it but really not be it or really be connected to what you're doing while doing it. Identification matters. Say it with me "**identification matters**." Identification is so important, and your identification (in the spirit) must be always carried with you. You're obligated no matter what to walk in who Christ has identified you to be in Him.

But!! You have to know who that person is first. The reason why you've got to know who you are in Him is because there will be something or someone that will come to challenge who you believe you are and/or who He called you to be.

These two are written separate because you could be someone in Christ and not have agreed with it yet. Also known as an "*identity crisis*". A secured identity is also a solidified identity.

Jesus' first encounter with the woman at the well involved Him asking for something. Jesus asked the woman for a drink. Her response posed a question of her identification because she goes on to describe who both she and Jesus were.

So, one of the distinctions you will need early in your identification process is how you hear from God as well as how He deals with you. This knowledge will assist you in embracing who you are.

There have been times in my life especially recently that I was so broken that I didn't feel the worthiness to ask God for anything substantial even when I knew that I had a moment in His presence where I could have very well asked Him for anything. Most of the time in His presence we spend casting all of our burdens, asking for more stuff and leaving refreshed. But when was the last time you spent time with the Father and didn't ask Him for a thing? Identification in Christ is an exchange. Identification in Christ requires what you have of yourself for what He can give of Himself. Our ultimate goal is to look and to be like Him.

Identification requires full knowledge of the track record of God. It's our doubt in our encounters with the Father that cause us to be ignorant in His total ability to fill us, replenish us and top us off if needed. He is literally all that we will ever need.

It's this (our doubt in His ability) that ultimately cause us to question who we are. When your relationship with Him is questionable who you are and even who you believe you are will be skewed as well.

The first layer to dig through after your discipline is established is in your identification because you have to distinguish what God is doing in your entire being simply by being in His presence. You will never feel like enough when you don't know who you are. Ever! So, a good starting place is asking Him for those things that will sustain you and keep you, all while (if needed) receiving the right identity. In the moments where your identity is being fixed ask also that you never thirst again for what is beneath you, what means you no good and what can't satisfy you. Because ultimately you have to know and be assured that only **HE** satisfies.

Today I will: Dig deeper!

☐ Who is God saying I am?

☐ Do I have the proper Identification?

☐ Why?

☐ You will never feel like or feel that you are enough without a Christ like image attached.

In the end:

You are Enough!

Dear Beautiful Soul:

Most of the time when you're out of the will of God and His purpose for your life you should look closely at your identity.

A fractured identity will cause you great grief. It's also highly visible to the outside eye. What has helped me of late isn't running to receive counsel or asking who "they" think I am or what "they" see me doing with my skill set but it's been time in prayer. The beauty of Christ and having a relationship with Him is He is the best secret keeper. I caution you though to not just come and dump on Him in the areas where you suffer in your identity without also being ready to receive the solution for all of it.

That means mind renewal and mind reversal. Retraining and rewiring all that you have been taught and all that is housed within.

Talk to yourself, I do all the time. Take a good look at yourself, not just for selfie with good lighting or because you're made up real nice. This look may have to be a first thing in the morning look and preferably a look in the mirror. You choose how just look! We are receiving a new identification and you won't even recognize the person in the picture. This is your foundation, and this is one of the most important phases you will need to work through. You should be able to answer without any doubt "who am I?".

3,2,1 ready the flash is on and your new I.D is on the way. You, beautiful soul are enough.

Dear Abba:

Section 2:
ACCEPTANCE

"As you read this, this is the day when the one who is enough simply says enough!"

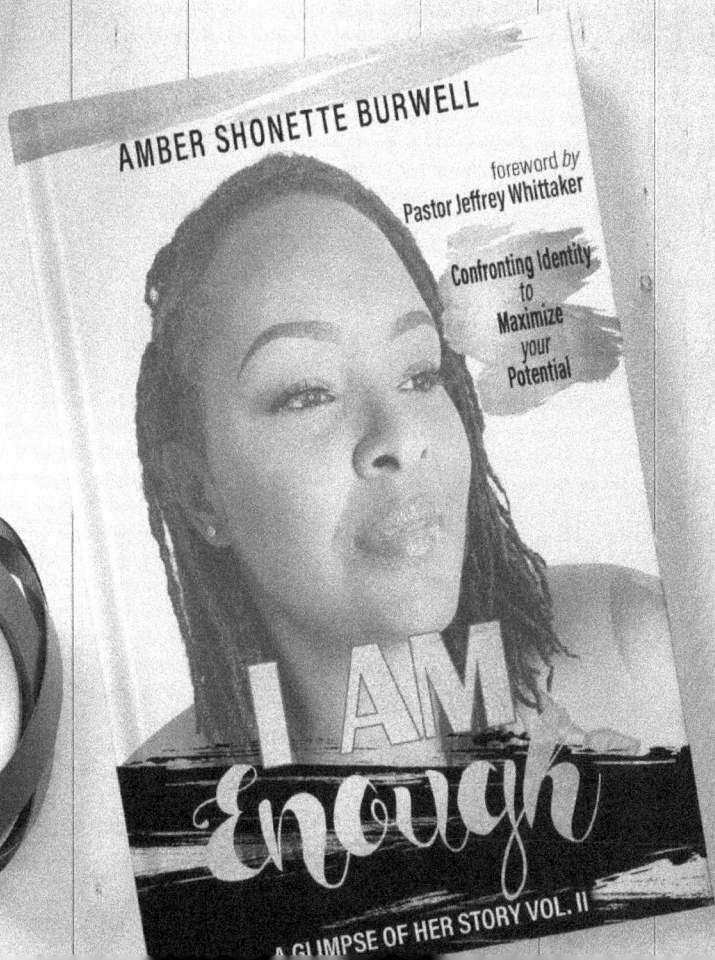

AMBER SHONETTE BURWELL

foreword by
Pastor Jeffrey Whittaker

Confronting Identity
to
Maximize
your
Potential

I AM
Enough

A GLIMPSE OF HER STORY VOL. II

ENOUGH IS ENOUGH

It is finished! I can't take it anymore. In fact, I am fed up and unsure of what is next but what I do know is that I have had it with where I am. How many times have we let this thinking and this kind of posture be what drove us either deeper over the edge or in some cases it drove us into our destiny? I pose two choices because I don't have to tell you that all we're up against and faced with in our lives is a matter of choice. The choice a long with the consequences ultimately are all ours.

It is the drive that we feel in this kind of moment however, that is the fuel that we need to push us into some of the greatest moments of our lives or the fumes that have us relying on external situations and people for survival. When you read the term "***enough is enough***" it has a negative connotation and can even cause your mind to go back to a time when you actually felt like this. What if I told you that today as you read this that this is the day when the one who is enough (you) simply said enough. Period. That we're not going to use this to thrust us into negativity and/or sin but this is going to be our framework and blueprint that we build upon throughout this book.

For the last 8 years I have been unmarried. And for the last 8 years I have been striving to become whole and healed, often having to go back, access and make hard admissions that some things still sting and the admission that other things still hurt. I married in my early 20's and I had no clue about dating, relationships, waiting on God, abstaining with purpose and on and on (here I was thinking it was the other party that was the problem). The one constant of my knowledge of who I was, was that there was a huge hole in my heart and a big void that I thought a relationship could fill and my gifts would be enough to cover ignoring my character flaws. Some days these 8 years feel like 80 years and other days they in no way compared to the 21 years that I spent in my own skin prior to marrying in 1997 and knowing Jesus. I can't say that this book and the lessons since my last book have been easy to digest but I will say they all have been necessary.

For me it was a combination of all the above scenarios I described that got me here writing about being enough and shifted the original direction I was going in. I was trying, trying to date, trying to move on and trying to be over healing in specific areas. In that, I finally caught the revelation that if a person or a group of people don't desire me, string me a long or refuse to see my value that doesn't make me any less desirable or valuable.

What it does mean (my light bulb moment) is they're not assigned to me for longevity, and they possibly weren't sent in my life by the Father, and that's ok. It has to be okay within. Of course, this could be highly related to male/female relationships but for intellect's sake not limited to just those type of relationships. This is **ANYONE** in your life. Anyone!
This doesn't mean that the people who are sent and supposed to be shouldn't confront me or tell me hard things it just means that I won't ever question someone desiring to depart out of my life.

So, what I found myself doing in order to try to make ill motives right I tried to fit a particular person in the jigsaw puzzle of my life. You know when you're down to what may feel like the last few pieces of a puzzle and you take pieces that you know don't fit (but they look like they will) and you press firmly, you press some more but there's something that feels off which causes you to (hopefully) decide (oftentimes with disappointment) that it's just not going to work. Find your fit and find what works for you but never force a fit.

Wait! Did you hear me say ill motives? What does that mean and have to do with all of this? So glad you asked. A while back in my devotion time I started an index card with "motives". You know what your motives are, they're your why but deeper than that I went into my heart (which we will talk about later) and then wrote down my why. I didn't really like that place. I didn't like how my motives made me feel in moments of uncertainty and desperation. I am just being honest.

This though, has been my point of reference and where I start. Why now? Why do I want what I want and why am I even here in God's presence? I am a vessel refined and renewed with all of the right intentions, right? To my core yes but at times when the heat is turned up, no. It is proving or the feeling of having to do so which has caused me to want to rush a season and/or a process sent to truly catapult me not to another level of giftedness and reward but a new level of character. Oh yes! My gifts aren't going anywhere but without the character to sustain said gifts I would surely die before I reap a harvest. What a tragedy that would be.

Goodness begets goodness and more goodness. You're going to see it! After gathering this type of revelation, the right thing to do is to access and gather the lesson of course, to look back on what happened to look at when and where things went wrong and how the breach occurred. More so have the character and integrity that match the level I am believing to be ascended to. It's these times when we look at our own reflection and stare hard (or we should). When we are on our knees and our faces crying out for answers to our good Father.

Throughout this book you will see "**I am enough**" until you get it, until you feel it and most importantly until you believe it.
For purposes of this chapter, I want to declare to you that yes! Enough is Enough. Enough of what has held you back, enough of what has caused you to question why? And enough of the parts of you that refuse to let go. Enough!!!

Today I will: Dig deeper!

☐ Access any ill motives.

☐ Access any breach in my character.

☐ Why?

☐ Enough is enough and in the end:

You are enough!

Dear Beautiful Soul:

Hey! People get on our nerves sometime, right? Feels like your nerves have been trampled on. Can you relate? Of course, you can. Most of the time you're justified in how you feel. *It hurt, it wasn't necessary, and it made you feel some type of way. I get it! To add you just want one person (maybe two) to understand YOU AND HOW YOU FEEL. I get that too!*

Let's say you have the above, now what? Do you feel any better or more like the victim? A victim? That's not what you're looking to accomplish right you just want to be understood and maybe expose those that didn't understand you along the way.

Accepting or not it still makes you a victim. While I never want to disregard and discredit anyone's feelings, I want you to put death to the victim mentality and rethink how you view what and who hurt you. That's it.
Enough is Enough it's time for fresh perspective. You beautiful soul are enough.

Dear Abba:

"Until your heart is made new, you'll never see beyond the darkness of your past and the dawning of a new day."

A NEW HEART

When I wrote volume one I developed a great love for hearts (the symbol). In fact, I created a brand behind the Purple Heart to the "survivor" and the one who made it. Recently I have also included in post the black and/or the red heart and there of course is meaning behind this as well. The black heart symbolizing our pain, and the red heart being the blood of Jesus that is able to cleanse, clean and change any type of heart. More than just loving the symbol and the different colors I can use on my phone I have realized that the affinity I have is to the actual heart of a person that I love as well.

Today I consider myself very chill and mild mannered, but I wasn't always like this. For a long time, my story made me hard and extremely bitter. Perspective was the last thing I wanted to have regarding it and mercy and grace wasn't what I sought to give. If you hurt me, you would know it. That's not how it's supposed to be though. I imagine if I were to be treated like that by my heavenly Father how I would feel, and I also imagine if I never were given the opportunity to have a heart transplant how would I be?

Despite being bitter and traumatized I realized under all of that lay an extremely huge heart that was always willing to "try again". Whew! I have made many sacrifices as a single mom (often weary at times) and while doing so (my love for my children and grandchildren) also expanded my heart. I didn't always make the right decisions because of bitterness and because I at one point saw no way out of my circumstance. Finding balance for me has been an ongoing task. I will do anything for those that I love and with that it has caused me great resentment for having such a process etched in my story. I have not always known how and when to draw the line. A deep lover often hurts deeply as well.

With all of this I know now my heart has been made new and it's even shifted in the thoughts and beliefs that I was reared on and those that assisted in shaping and molding me. My heart is my hub, my command center and quality control at certain times is necessary.

You see until your heart is made new, you'll never feel like you're enough, or satisfied with yourself. Until your heart is made new, you'll never see beyond the darkness of your past and the dawning of a new day. Simply put you will **NEVER LET GO**. I am super grateful for the depth and even expansion in my heart muscles to include more people, more creativity and more sunshine but more grateful for a surgeon and the desperate need I had to receive a new heart. I caution you that you will be adjusting (or you should be) with your new heart to adapt and to take on the nature and characteristics of Christ. The adversary will try to plant lies that you're soft and being walked on.

Don't listen. Aside from that, however, is a new heart functioning and operating to perfect all that you house all that your destiny holds. You see the fact that your heart is now new is proof of just how amazing you are, just how much you are enough! How much stamina you have, and the grace placed on your life.

Today I will: Dig deeper!

☐ Search my old heart.

☐ Receive a new heart.

☐ Why?

☐ Depth and expansion require a new heart.

In the end:

You are enough!

Dear Beautiful Soul:

I see your heart and others do too. Sometimes nurtured other times neglected. You're too precious to carry around all that you do. You're far too valuable to be weighed down. I can't tell you the number of times I have had to "check my heart". I can't tell you the number of times I have had to go back to the drawing board and start over. Nor can

I recall the number of times when I had to make the hard admission that the wound, the offense, the pain still stung. Yep! After such an admission I then had to also ask myself why I allowed "them" to even get through all my externals and into my heart into my sacred place.

So, what I had to do in those moments is make the determination that I not only played a role, but I allowed them in. I had to make the determination that I entertained and welcomed whatever "it" was. I also learned in these moments that it was quite possible that I had made my way through layers of someone's heart and hurt them deeply as well.

This particular letter isn't all about the "bad" and the "pain", but it is to let you know that what makes its way to your heart must be dealt with and or compartmentalized. Your heart is so precious, so fragile and so rare.
You my friend (big heart and all) are enough!

Dear Abba:

"Yes, is more than saying "yes I am enough". It's saying God I agree with the direction you have me going in, where you're taking me and how you're navigating to assure I get there."

YOUR YES

One of the sure ways your "I am enough" declaration is solidified is by coming into agreement with who God says you are (identification), and by believing it no matter what you see or your past mistakes. The simplest way to agree with all of it is by saying "yes". That seems obvious but yes is a heart posture before it's muttered out of your mouth. Your yes will typically cost you something that may be near and dear to you.

The reason why I titled this chapter "your yes" is because with all the power and strength that the word yes holds you first need to know and accept that it's personal (it's all yours). Your yes is binding and holds you to Gods standard over your life. Your yes says "God I agree with you" and your yes says you accept what God is doing (in, through and around you) although you may not understand it all.

I know that because I have struggled with being enough and in my identity that I have in turn struggled with my yes, as it relates to my current state and my destiny. I have given a yes that I knew my heart either didn't want to give or was bitter toward giving. This has stunted my progress I know for a fact. Of late, I have been making it a better practice not to be swayed or even controlled by my emotions. Therefore, when saying yes (for me) it's not necessarily all about agreement but has been about being sober in my thinking and understanding that what I have to let go of God is able to replenish in another form. My yes has been a battle at times, and I have had to see it beyond coming to torment me and cause me harm. A firm yes will not do those rather it will catapult and send you to where you're supposed to be.

So here yes is more than saying "yes I am enough". It's saying God I agree with the direction you have me going in, where you're taking me and how you're navigating to assure I get there.

This is a time in our lives where we will be strengthened with a heartfelt yes, we'll be empowered, and we will overcome doubt, fear and

adversity. All with one word and that word is yes.
Disclaimer: if you're not ready that's okay this chapter and devotional will be here for you when you're ready.

Today I will: **Dig deeper!**

☐ Say yes to God! And mean it.

☐ Agree with where God is taking you via your yes.

☐ Why?

☐ In order to thrive you'll have to give God a heartfelt yes.!

In the end:

You are enough!

Dear Beautiful Soul:

I can see how yes often times can be associated with pain. The pain of mustering up the strength to say it then having to live through the disappointment and the letdown of it not panning out quite the way you planned, or even envisioned. That is our problem. Holding a yes to God in the same way we would hold a yes to a person. They don't hold the same weight. *So, I want to inspire you and maybe nudge you a little that this yes is chock full of next level for you, this yes will fuel you but above all: this yes is* necessary. *This is actually the one you've been holding on to.*

You see a sure yes gives you more arsenal in your identity tool kit and in this context, it takes the sting out of, can I? will I? or am I enough? You are, you know that, and you always have been but your yes needs your fight and your allegiance. That is one of the missing keys.

Take this time, take this entry and take your experiences all while saying yes! It's time for real one! You beautiful soul are enough!

Dear Abba:

Section 3:
THE WELL

"If you find yourself face to face with Jesus you're right where you need to be."

DEPTH

My original direction was going to be around the story of the woman at the well. I found that my story had a few significant similarities that were worth highlighting. When the direction shifted, I knew I could still talk about her and not loose what I was conveying in this work. One piece of her story worth mentioning is that in all she had going on she was thirsty. She had "*needs*" however, she had a life changing encounter in spite of the ugly and misunderstood parts of her story.

Why write about and talk about depth? What's it all about? Well in my opinion this woman had to do some digging or modern-day term "soul searching" in the moment and during her encounter with the Father. Her wells because of all she had endured (5 husbands) were deep.

There are times when your well is extremely deep that it can become contaminated. In other words, someone may walk by (or come into your life) and throw something useless (or what they deem not valuable to them) in it and you become filled with lots of junk. Then you have to stop and deal with that deposit. It's a vicious cycle that will continue if you don't stop letting people do *drive bye's* and *drop offs.*

I have been extremely thirsty before, not just relating to the opposite sex or the desire to have someone but generally. My mantra was if I had more of this, more of that my thirst would be quenched. But you do know the wrong type of quenching can make you thirstier? That was me filling up on so much of what I thought I needed and wanted all while water from the Father was waiting for me and everlasting too.

I would say I am deep and have depth. Not deep in that I'm not relatable but a deep lover, a deep thinker (and an over thinker at times) and a feeler. I have been in situations before where I can "feel" before anything if something is off. But my depth in various situations proved a great level of shallowness whereas I was deceived, manipulated and taken advantage of. These led to compromising and questioning on actually being enough and overachieving.

I had to access the depth of my well(s). In other words, how did I get here and how ultimately could I get out of this without looking like what I have been through. The Woman at the Well had depth to her. The depth she spoke about was the depth of her well and all that resided there. Much of what we need and much of what we have to attend to in our souls need the touch and balm that only Jesus can provide but because of pride, arrogance and stubbornness we cause ourselves great suffering. Our wounds and our pain feel as though not even Jesus Himself has what we need. Feels like they are bigger than the problem solver. What a lie. It is the contrary, if you find yourself face to face with Jesus you're right where you need to be. BUT! You have got to go in deep. You have to immerse every part of yourself in deeply with Him. Trust Him, He can handle it. In fact, He's been waiting for the moment you realize that He is not just the one bringing you to the living water you need, living water is who He is.

What's happening in you will require a dig to even the parts that have been deemed off limits, the parts that have been suppressed and the parts that have been forgotten about. Why? Because now you're headed into the place where communion lies as well as solutions and answers. The deep place of God is in His presence. Just you and the Father! The way it was truly designed to be.

Today I will: Dig deeper!

- [ ] Into each and every well.

- [ ] When I have gone deep, I will go deeper.

- [ ] Why?

- [ ] It's the pathway and the road to living water.!

In the end:

You are enough!

Dear Beautiful Soul:

I know that the dig can be painful, but the dig is what clears the way for something new to come in. I know how when you think back in your mind you wonder how you made it through with a well filled with so much pain and a well that had so many taking from you. I get it! Look at the great exchange that has taken place. A loving and gracious Father that knows all you endured yet still He decided to flush out and to pour into you His living water. How amazing!

You're deep and that's okay but the love, the mercy and the grace of Abba is deeper. As you read this as you ponder this know that because of the unfailing favor over your life, you my friend are enough! Now that's deep and that's depth!

Dear Abba:

"If your taste buds are feasting on the world, if your identity is tied up in others and what they're doing and if you feel less than because of others, chances are your appetite needs an adjustment and fast."

APPETITES

I have learned so much about appetites both naturally and spiritually. The right appetite for the right things long enough will create great discipline. You have to keep doing a thing and eventually you will **want** to do it also. It takes time.

It has been hard during a national pandemic to have the appetite for the right things all of the time (naturally). What I have learned however, through this is that there comes a time when you have to let your flesh know who is in control. It was becoming quite obvious to me (and the scale) that I was constantly craving the wrong things. I still will say I still can do better, but I am doing better than I was.

I am reminded of the scripture that says that Jesus' appetite is to do the will of the one who sent him (John 5:30). In other words, His desire was for righteousness and to conform to what the

Father wills. If not, just like in the natural your spiritual appetites that aren't healthy will cause you to become sick.

The way you see yourself either being enough or not enough is tied to what you feed yourself (spiritually) and eventually digest. You can also look at it from a natural perspective because too much of the wrong things naturally will most certainly skew your view of yourself and cause you to feel like less than what you really are and who God says you are.
So, one of the key areas of your appetite in feeling, being and knowing you're enough, is to get a tight grip on your flesh.

Too much time in the flesh leaves less time for the spiritual things of God to be prominent in your life. I don't know how many times I have put more trust than I needed to in my flesh, and in my own will power. Not realizing that the true test of my ability to endure what the flesh was bringing my way was just that – a test. I needed to know that I was truly overcoming by my ability to say no to **what I wanted**. This isn't just limited when you talk about the flesh to sexual gratification but anything you crave more than you crave God can be considered a fleshly issue and an idol. Status, platforms, career moves and your bag just to name a few.

A way to starve the appetite for those areas and more is to spend time with the Father. Doing so helps you not only to crave the right things but to begin to desire them also. If your taste buds are feasting on the world, if your identity is tied up in others and what they're doing and if you feel less than because of others, chances are your appetite needs an adjustment and fast. Your flesh only rules over you if you let it. You can win the battle within and in your flesh by changing your appetite.

Today I will: Dig deeper!

☐ Into the right appetites

☐ In the spirit and not after the flesh.

☐ Why?

☐ It's most satisfying.

In the end:

You are enough!

Dear Beautiful Soul:

Nothing like something that taste good but isn't good by any means for you. *I know this all too well. Desiring to do what was right and unfortunately not having the heart, the discipline or the prayer life to sustain any of it. More of the wrong things and time spent outside of God's presence the more it will be like the "regular gas" on a luxury car. Sure, you'll have the fuel and even move but eventually you will possibly damage your vehicle and in this example your soul.*

It is time to check your (spiritual) diet, and time to check what you crave. Your taste buds are keeping you from having the right harvest and from reaping Gods way. Much of what you have feasted on has kept you from enjoying pure bliss when it comes to Gods will for your life.

Sure, you see nothing wrong presently, but you will look years down the line with a heart full of regret wondering how you spent all of this time eating, digesting and eating again the wrong things entirely. You can't go out like that because you are enough!

Dear Abba:

Section 4:
AFFIRMATION

"No, you can't go back and change what happened and what you didn't have but you can make sure that limiting yourself because of devastation won't be in your story."

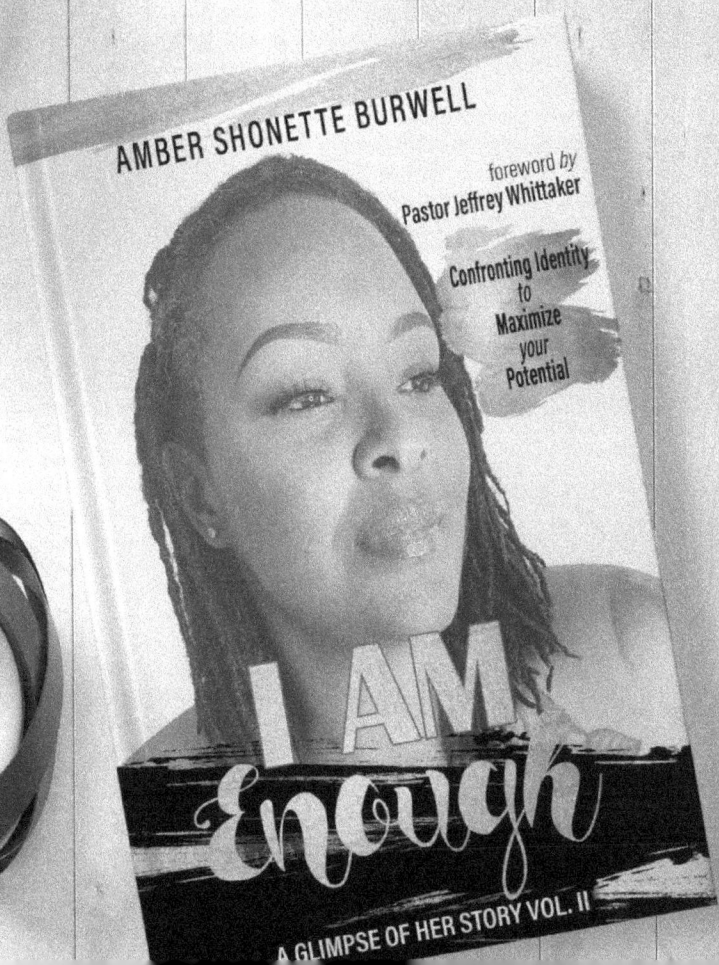

AMBER SHONETTE BURWELL

foreword *by* Pastor Jeffrey Whittaker

Confronting Identity to Maximize your Potential

I AM Enough

A GLIMPSE OF HER STORY VOL. II

WHO TOLD YOU THAT?

One of my struggles in life not just in being enough but in general came from lack of affirmation. I am always extremely grateful to God for these types of revelations in my life because it means I have defeated a huge part of what has tried to defeat me. How so? Because I know the problem. You should try it by simply acknowledging what the Lord reveals to you especially when it comes to your healing, growth, development and your evolution.

Affirmation is defined as affirming something, but it's also defined as emotional support or encouragement. All my life I have struggled with affirmation, all my life I have struggled with wanting to be accepted and wanting to prove to those close to me that I was somebody. I also managed to really care about others perception of me as well. Hindsight of course has shown me this is why I also have suffered with extreme fear when speaking publicly, anxiety over things that haven't happened (but I created scenarios in my head), and I have talked myself out of things and opportunities I know were God and that He told me to do.

It felt easier and comfortable to just isolate myself, not do it so I wouldn't have an "I failed" testimony attached to it.
The question is and becomes when did it get in deep enough that I started to believe it? In other words, who told me (and you) that? A severe identity crisis whether it be lack of affirmation or not starts off as a belief and what you believe about yourself.

This year (2020) I turned 44 and one of the things I became decided in was to stop limiting myself and even talking myself out of hard things. Not hard just from a labor perspective but what wasn't natural for me. Example: If I didn't do "it" 5 years ago why did "it" suddenly become a hard no and no longer could be done? One answer is comfort will have you settling, ease will have you coasting on the same level for years and one-track perspective will cause you to never see more, see beyond and aim to go there. Not anymore.

I decided to work on some aesthetic insecurities, talk to myself, ask for help and start working on helping others that struggle with the same things I do. AND I'm not waiting until a husband comes, or all my ducks are lined up. I am going to prayerfully do what God is pushing me to do. But I can't alone. I need you to do so too. Tomorrow may never come, the deal of a lifetime might not either, but your impact can be heard and felt beyond your lifetime if you establish that if someone told you and spoke over you or maybe they didn't (voices in your head are loud sometime too) it doesn't matter. If you were affirmed a lot or a little coming up that doesn't matter either because you have and serve a great God who desires to give you nothing but good things, you're going to obey His command and His voice alone. No, you can't go back and change what happened and what didn't have but you can make sure that limiting yourself because of devastation won't be in your story. Not today! You're too special for that, you are enough.

Today I will: Dig deeper!

☐ Grasp the hard revelation of my story.

☐ I will acknowledge it.

☐ Why?

☐ It doesn't matter what "they" told me and you.!

In the end:

You are enough!

Dear Beautiful Soul:

I am starting to think that "they" get too much credit. "They" take up too much space in your head and you have believed their lies for far too long. I get it, you're not perfect and "they" may even know some secrets of yours, but it doesn't matter. You have put too much work in to being a new creature to entertain the words, the lies and even the facts any longer. I want you to move past all of that because it has been literally crippling you. So where do you begin? By having hard conversations with the Father. In fact, I want you to consider on the next page getting it all out on paper. Some you may not want to hear some you may not remember. But once you face it with Him you won't have to entertain their words ever again. I promise.

Yes, they told you some things and you didn't get the affirmation you so desperately needed but that said and done, you're still enough.

Dear Abba:

"Sure, the temptation will be there to cave in and crumble, but we all have to get to a point in our lives where we're as consistent alone and/or in private as we are in front of people."

WHEN NO ONE SEES YOU

I am sure you have heard the saying that character is who you are when no one is looking. This could be said also for how you value yourself as well (being enough).

The reason for this is because you have to rely on strength and encouragement sometimes just from God. I remember writing (in volume one) that if no one saw the change in me or threw me a change party I was determined to make the arms (of God) my altar. In other words, you have got to keep doing the right thing when the right thing doesn't feel conducive or even when the opposite of the right thing is more easily accessible.

This doesn't just show you how valuable you are, but it also will cause you to affirm yourself as well, to even push yourself and encourage yourself. It will really show where your heart truly lies in what you're committed to and what you've been called to do. It will really prove to yourself and the one(s) watching (because someone is always watching) that you really believe you are enough. Sure, the temptation will be there to cave in and crumble, but we all have to get to a point in our lives where we're as consistent alone and/or in private as we are in front of people. We not only have to be delivered from people, but we also have to at times divert ourselves from their attention and applauds. Otherwise, it will cause us to rely on them more than God.

When we look at being free from people, we can also look at several roots attached to that as well. I know and I have had to learn how to have conversation in my personal time with God that helps to ease those moments when I feel the need to "be seen". It has helped me tremendously and really humbled me.

My advice? You'll still make it, and you'll still have what it takes even when you're faced with what you did and accomplished behind the backs of those that never saw you. Always know no matter what that your value has been already established even when "no one sees you".

The God that you serve sees all and knows all and the platforms that we aspire to have or even gain come from Him. That is what I am experiencing: and have even been told in my prayer time. Platforms aren't given as a byproduct of promotion, but platforms are given when you're postured. Keep going, the timing of God is oh so perfect.

Today I will: Dig deeper!

☐ Beyond the "they" in my life.

☐ Have close communion and conversation with God.

☐ Why?

☐ He's building me in places when no one sees me.!

In the end:

You are enough!

Dear Beautiful Soul:

Sure, the credit is great, the acknowledgement too but your focus should be too and is greater. Focus on the inside, what is happening internally because of the closed curtains, the alone time and even the relationships that you thought you needed that ended. You need this, it's necessary and in the end, this will be of great benefit to you. This will be your tipping point to get over people and also the moment you learn how to protect your peace.

I decree great peace and great humility over you as you finally see your value beyond who's looking. Either way! You are enough.

Dear Abba:

Section 5:
ADORATION

"In your pursuit of and acceptance of being enough you have got to balance the love of and discipline of God in YOUR LIFE!!"

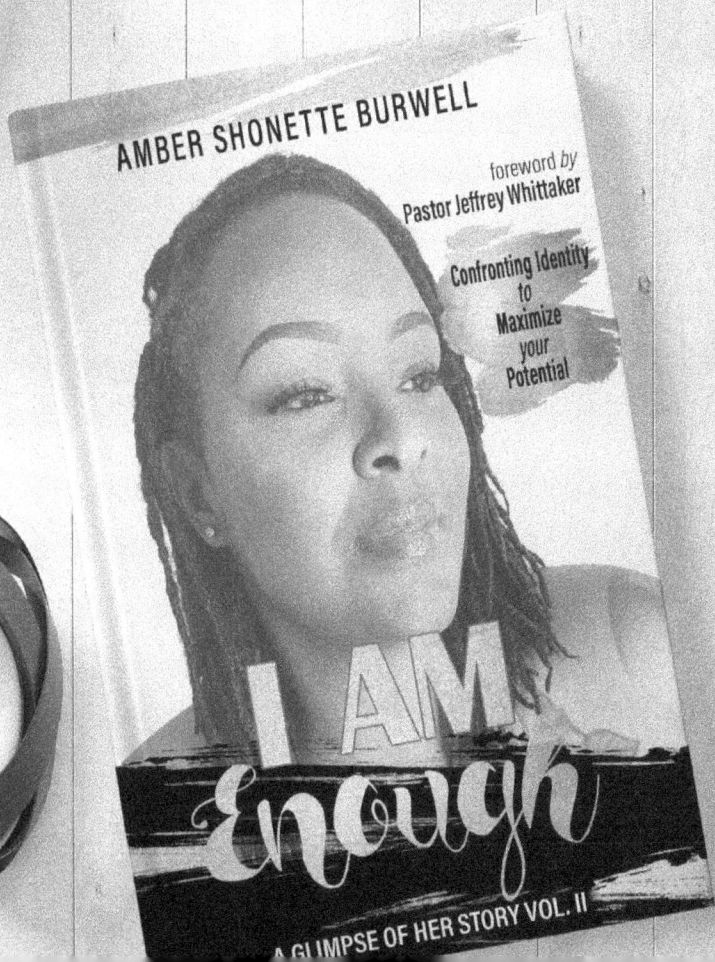

AMBER SHONETTE BURWELL

foreword by
Pastor Jeffrey Whittaker

Confronting Identity
to
Maximize
your
Potential

I AM
Enough

A GLIMPSE OF HER STORY VOL. II

THOSE HE LOVES

When I wrote my first book and pondered sharing some of the situations of my life for the first time what stood out a lot was not just my difference but feeling the weight of that difference in my early years. As I am writing this chapter what now stands out is God's love for me. Often when people of God share the word of the Lord with me concerning me or anything concerning me, I would hear "God loves you". It's true if you hear something long enough you should (hopefully) start to believe it.

I feel the love of God often in my life and in times of great loneliness or when the adversary still tries to remind me that I'm not married and will never be. I laugh now although it will seek to try to stay with me (the thought of not being married again) and continue doing what I know to do and what is right in the eyes of God.

Throughout my 44 years of life, it's not been easy and some of that realization was disobedience in many areas. I feel like and I know had I stuck to the plan and walked it out it would have gone another way. I am reminded of Hebrews 12:6 (ESV) which says, "for the lord disciplines those he loves, and he chastises every son whom he receives."

It's so true you will find the love of God wrapped up in His chastisement and also uncover the standard on your life too. You can't just do and get away with any ol' thing or have a go with the flow attitude because of what others do and get away with and it seems like with ease the Lord will check you on.

In your pursuit of and acceptance of being enough you have got to balance the love of and discipline of God in YOUR LIFE!! You have got to know what the fruit of His Spirit is which may require you to produce under pressure. You have got to kill the notions and stories in your head that suggest perfection and the ones that suggest that you won't be tried while serving the Lord. Those notions don't exist and seek to create great frustration within. If you cling to and have moments in the presence of the Lord where you feel and are reassured of His love you will know that anything that is happening in and around, you will ultimately serve a greater purpose for you.

That is what happens when you have a revelation of "those He loves" down pact. You will recognize and accept that the love He has for you will cause Him to make executive decisions on your behalf not only for you but because of your purpose, your present and because of your destiny.

Today I will: Dig deeper!

☐ Into Gods love for me.

☐ Beyond perfection and ease.

☐ Why?

☐ You will begin to accept the path you're on with Him.!

In the end:

You are enough!

Dear Beautiful Soul:

Love is strong and powerful, isn't it? I am sure you haphazardly tossed this word around a few times in your life. I am sure you made comparison to the one you thought you loved and loved you to Gods love for you. I know you found or maybe you're still learning they're not the same.

The bible tells us that God loves us with an everlasting love. In fact, it's His love that often keeps us going because you know you right? (You know how you are) And you know that He should have given up on you a long time ago. He didn't. In
His love and in the correction, you have faced with Him you have got to know that it has all been factored in and apart of the plan for your life.

His love won't ever change. You can't disconnect from it or do anything that would cause Him to love you less. Not only because you're His child but because you are enough!

Dear Abba:

HONOR

I think that a huge part of seeing yourself in the right reflection of being enough is how well you do honor. Sure, this means how well you honor people, but it also means how well you honor yourself. This is a major key to being enough and really meaning it. By honor we mean your time, your body, your space and even access. I have struggled in all of those areas but especially in the area of access. Giving access to another not realizing access is earned and not deserved and granted to everyone. I have literally burned my candle at both ends by allowing myself to be drained and taken advantage of my giving away access.

You have got to honor yourself and you have also got to forgive yourself. It's a must. Regret and bitterness will eat away at you and cause you to become stuck in a moment of time that has long gone away. You can't charge yourself for the knowledge only obtained after the storm.

Forgive yourself. And assure yourself that in all things and all that was given to you and placed before you...you did your best! If you believe that and can say that let that marinate also and free you.
Honor those sent to you to speak hard things over your life. The good is easy but the hard comes from a place of love. Get accountability and get around someone that is willing to not just bring the best out in you but not stop grinding with you until it manifest.

Lastly, honor God. Honor Him currently, honor who He has been to you in past times. Honor Him with the fruit of an obedient life and a clean and pure heart. Honor Him by putting him first in everything that you do. Honor Him by the seat in your heart reserved just for Him. He is truly worthy of it all.

Today I will: Dig deeper!

☐ Make honor apart of my journey.

☐ Honor the Godly relationships in my life.

☐ Why?

☐ You must do honor well.!

In the end:

You are enough!

Dear Beautiful Soul:

Dishonor will always derail your destiny. Honor, however, will cause you to hone into the greatest parts of yourself and your story.

You have got to realize that honoring well will cause all to be well within. Honor all, honor when it's hard, and honor those that have gone on yet had a place in your life to shape and mold who you are.

Flourish in honor by honoring your time, your body, your resources and your life. Give the Father back all He is due. How? With glory and honor.

I honor you beautiful soul, you are enough.

Dear Abba:

Section 6:
BLOGS & DEVOTIONAL

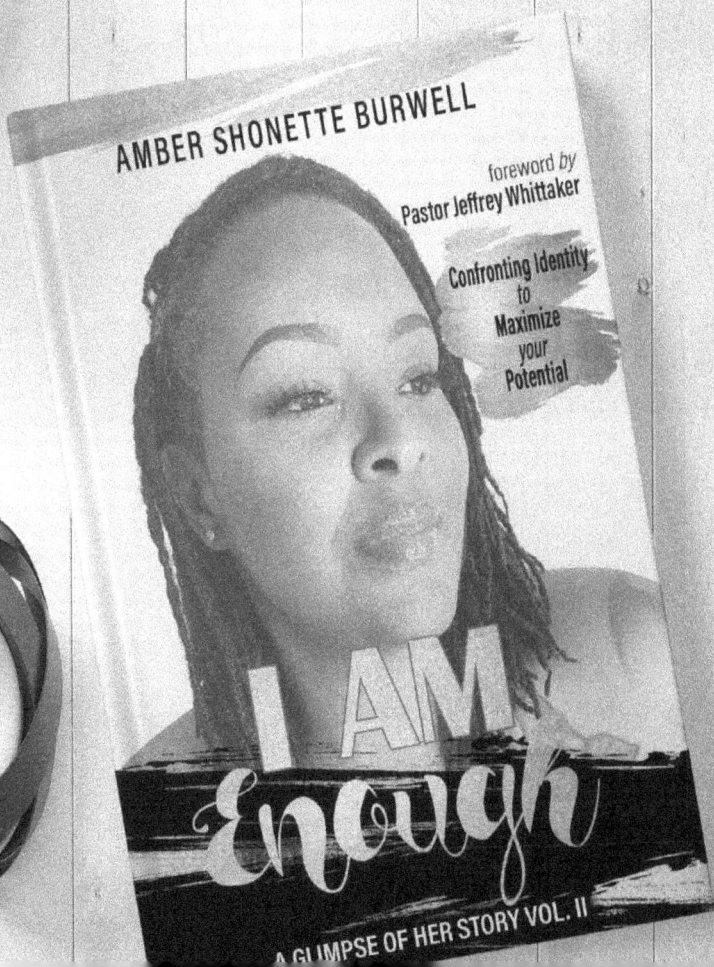

AMBER SHONETTE BURWELL

foreword *by*
Pastor Jeffrey Whittaker

Confronting Identity
to
Maximize
your
Potential

I AM
Enough

A GLIMPSE OF HER STORY VOL. II

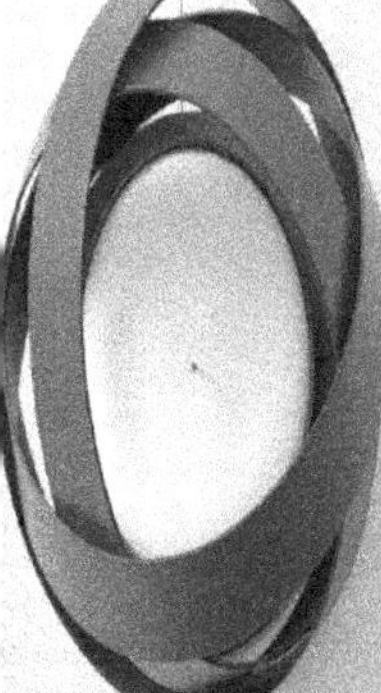

Life and Healing

I remember being at the peak of my inner healing journey. I was super focused and shedding many things that didn't belong. However, I've never had the opportunity to take all the time I needed to heal or lock myself in a room if I had to.

This is because for the duration of my journey I have been a single mom. I have always found myself responsible for something and having something going on.

I am so used to living a life of great responsibility that to be able to rest and reset sometimes seems foreign to me. However, I believe that there is a place of rest that must be sought in Christ to be able to balance healing and the pressures of life well.

During my time of healing, there was a moment when I became a little selfish. I was so determined to leap over the hurdle and curve the plateau I felt I had reached.

It was important to me that I saw and made it to a certain level in my journey. Therefore, it didn't matter that certain things went undone and overlooked.

Admittedly, I am not the best multi-tasker. I could be mid-sentence into a story and find myself checking an email or something else, pause my whole story, and lose my train of thought. I have a desire to do better in this area and to work on giving people my undivided attention

At times, it can be difficult to multi-task while healing. it can also be difficult when you're the 'go-to person' for everyone and the one who holds it all together.

During this moment of my journey, my godmother brought to my attention that although my intentionality was understandable, I had become too focused on just me and my selfishness was affecting my children.

So, I want to encourage anyone reading this that there will be times when you will have to balance life and healing. If done gracefully, nothing will suffer in and around you, but you must recognize the need and the importance of doing both interchangeably because both are necessary.

With Christ as our helper, we won't have to sacrifice the responsibilities of life or our healing. However, we must make it known to Him that we need him to lead us in balancing the two.

If you notice that life around you is spinning out of control, there could be a balance issue that you may need to address. Balancing the two may be difficult at times but remember there's nothing too hard or impossible with the Father. Let's go

Every day with Jesus

There shouldn't be a day that goes by that I am uncertain on what to do

Because all my days and a lot of my time should be spent w you.

There will never be a part of my story and/or my journey that you're not privy to

Because all my days and a lot of my time should be spent with you.

But reality has afforded me moments where grace had to foot the bill

Yet I'm wise enough to know: all my days and a lot of my time should be spent with you, STILL

So, I run to find you, looking all around, desperate, thirsty too.

But I KNOW I KNOW: all my days and a lot of my time should be spent with you

Admittedly I have chosen me instead

Knowing that at your feet is where I need to be fed

Where do I start? I have no clue

One thing's for sure that all my days and a lot of my time should be spent with you

To walk after the spirit means to turn from the very thing that would ultimately, please us.

The mind of the one who spends every day with Jesus

What I Saw

I looked in the mirror and took a deep breath
besides a few flaws, I liked what I saw

I looked at my clothes and removed all the tags I
put on my best
Hmmmm a few flaws but I liked what I saw
I got in my car; I ride real nice driving and flawed
but overall, I liked what I saw.

I arrived at my job, blessed by the best.
Although working and flawed I liked what I saw.

I arrived back home, what a day you brought me
through. Reminded of my flaws still I liked what I
saw.

Hold up its time for me to pray before the day gets
away. Able to cast my flaws so I can say I liked
what I saw.

While in prayer it was tough to go "there"
you assured me I was made for more so still able
to say I liked what I saw.

But there was something that had to be healed
something I had to finally sit and deal. My heart is

where you would start and as we sat and unpacked. It was here that in addition to my flaws I didn't like what I saw.

Accessing Rejection

Rejection. We all have experienced it. Unfortunately, when this happens it makes us instantly question ourselves.

It makes us ask why we weren't good enough and why we weren't the choice. But all of these questions we tend to ask ourselves are based on the other person's view and not our own or God's view of us.

Let's journey through this for a moment and hopefully find fresh perspective and clarity. We don't necessarily need another definition of what rejection is. It's fair to say that it's a denial and a dismissal. We have also heard that it's "God's protection."

When I hear the latter, I envision Holy Spirit doing an assessment on one's desire and deeming it an imperfect fit for you now or for your future. In this blog, we will deal mainly with how rejection in relationships impacts our inner healing journey.

Rejection, however, isn't limited to just male/female relationships. Rejection starts typically early on in life. When left untreated, rejection grows and ends in various cycles including sin and the need for deliverance.

In order to be totally healed, whole and unoffended in this area there are a few things that must be addressed. First, you must address your **perspective**.

You may be thinking there isn't really a perspective. I was rejected, the end! Correct, but the right perspective makes the sting and the trauma of anything less brutal. Having the right perspective is for the mature and causes one to ask hard questions.

Next, you will need to address your **pursuits**. Do your pursuits align with the voice of God and His word? Typically, when what we're pursuing or desiring doesn't align, we find ourselves rejected because God was never consulted.

Lastly, you'll have to look at your **passions**. This is your why and the motive behind your why.

The reason why all are important is because we could be self-inflicting all kinds of emotions on ourselves. This also may be God's way of revealing a level of healing that still needs to take place on the inside of you.

Pray for exposure of areas of suppression and areas that contain residue. Only a wounded and broken soul would continue to be persistent in an area that God has said was off-limits or that the ill intent of a person was already revealed. Doing so will cause you to continue to be controlled by the spirit of rejection, shame, confusion and frustration.

Live and Not Die

The fight for the future, introduces the war for the present.

Where I dwell often is certainly not what you meant,

When u said u came for Life and life more abundant

You came for assignments; I have to fulfill.

You came with better things including your sovereign and perfect will.

But there is an adversary who hates me to my core,

Allowed to test me often so in turn from you I need so much more.

Yes of course!!!

The fight for the future, introduces the war for the present.

Where I dwell often is certainly not what you meant,
When you said before I formed you, I knew you and I set you apart.

Yet I've been lonely, bitter and wounded.

Father purify my heart....

But wait there's more I thought I told depression she had to go.

Why does she make return trips as if I don't know?

Last time.

The fight for the future, introduces the war for the present.

Where I dwell often is certainly not what you meant,

When I see how you value and how deeply you love me.

We're here now daddy its literally above me.

The fight for the future, pause.

I give you all of me feel free to pry
Because you've given me words to heal me
Therefore, I WILL Live and not die…

HERSTORY!!!

God, I Trust You

My mantra, my solace.
The source of my existence.
My haven, my safety always so consistent.
My theme, my banner what seems to make the most sense.
My strength my wind what I chase w persistence
My quiet my devotion the steps that I take
No matter what is going on this I can't seem to shake
Seeking wisdom above things and knowledge above gain
One thing I desire, and this will always remain
Your peace and your presence when life seems to thrust me
Your voice in this season is "daughter just trust me".
So, I am finding in cases of uncertainty, cases of haste and cases when I want to rush
Heaven sends a message to my soul that in lieu of those what I need more is in my God to trust.
God, I trust you!

He Heals

The difference between self-reflection and introspection is one focuses on all of you and the other focuses on the emotional part of you. Once you understand this, you really can begin to plow and dig through various parts of your life.

Completion in these areas guarantees a treasure. These treasures come in the form of knowing who you really are, understanding the meaning of your life and noticing how the Lord has been with you all along. This can happen when you truly put in the work.

I went through this kind of process when I published my first book. Much of what I thought was dealt with or I healed from resurfaced.

What resurfaces especially when writing happens for authenticity sake. Pause here. You can only heal from (and assist someone in healing through) what you feel.

Even if you haven't directly been impacted by a thing, you have to feel it. If it doesn't become tangible and real to you in a moment you will never receive clearance spiritually.

Clearance ensures you move forward healthily. Give yourself permission to both feel and heal and do these at the same time. Then release all of the pain.

Prayerfully, you have settled the call on your life by now. Prayerfully, you have also settled that that call on your life has the lives of others attached to it.

I have previously blogged about forgiveness which I won't get into, but I will make mention after you feel and heal that you have to forgive yourself. Yes yourself! It is extremely important to clear yourself of others lodged in your heart including YOURSELF.

Some of this consist of the things you didn't know, the voids you tried to fill, the wisdom and knowledge that you were exempt from and not privileged to and the decisions you made with limited view and vision of the future.

Doesn't matter what else you could insert that was self-inflicted, you have to forgive yourself. You're not that person anymore and you deserve another chance to do it all again.

After you forgive yourself, you have to focus. Forward focus for the future is essential.

Eliminating distractions is a must. Eliminating distractions gives us clear perspective.

Let's recap! You're doing things differently this time around looking within, healing for real, forgiving yourself and becoming focused.

Finally! You have to have faith in the word of God and what it says concerning God's ability. The word is filled with promises, blessings and wisdom among other things, but we actually need moments where we meditate and study about the one who can do all things.

Psalm 147:3 starts like this, **He heals**. It says more of course, but "He heals" is a complete sentence.

Faith in the word gives you faith in the one who can execute and bring it to pass even when it looks like He can't. Your healing is super personal, but your healing also doesn't have a limit.

Give our Father your all as He administers the IV, the oxygen and whatever else you need to finally heal. You can trust Him.

Not A Man

Your life now in spite of where you are is being held together by a revelation. What that means is that you know there is much more to enjoy, possess and experience than your current state. When you have a revelation of a thing it can bring on a degree of healing, wholeness and tremendous joy in your life. Revelation is the thing that can cause us to see ourselves through the eyes of Christ vs. how people see us. Revelation enhances vision. Revelation is why you haven't given up. Revelation is what you're standing on.

We all (if we have accepted Christ) have some kind of revelation of who Jesus is. Some of it is based on word of mouth but a lot of it is based on relationship and fellowship with Him. Sometimes we do ourselves a great disservice by neglecting true intimacy with Christ and only settling for a surface level relationship which in turn can taint our revelation of Him. The reason why this can ultimately be harmful to us is our relationship can get stored and classified with all the other relationships we have with (hu)mans.

I have been single for a while now and it's been in my singleness (post-divorce) that I made the discovery about how important inner healing is. In my attempts to meet men, move forward and begin again I have been told on various occasions about the walls that are evidently present in me. I can only speak for me, but I know someone else would agree that it's not the intent to make someone new pay for what someone old did. BUT!!! It happens all the time. In our efforts and pursuits to not experience something (that happened before) we hope that our protection will also preserve us, but that is a sad reality and often not the case.

Let's switch to worship. I have felt and experienced the same battles and walls as I have tried to press in and worship corporately. There should not be feelings of worry, fear, anxiety or wondering what others are thinking about you in worship. It's this kind of battle that defeats the true purpose and your ultimate break through.

Both scenarios listed above have one thing in common how we not only limit God in what He can do in us, but we also place human standards, limitations and expectations on Him. God is not like (hu)mans (Numbers 23:19). This is the knowledge that begins to aid us in removing Him from painful situations and the box we have put Him in. He's not that person, or what they did,

He's not that trauma or that disappointment. He has to be placed above it so that we can recognize Him as the one with the power and authority over it and the antidote and the balm that will relieve it.

While we thank God for revealing to us Himself and His son there is nothing more liberating than the revelation that He isn't like a man or a man. God is greater than.

Soul Goals

Inner healing is multi-faceted and a complex journey. If you get caught up in comparing where you are versus where someone else is, you will not only become frustrated, but you can also become distracted in your personal pursuit of wholeness.

During the process of addressing what needs to be dealt with internally, it's easy to define ourselves by our small victories, titles and successful works. As a result of this, we can become trapped into thinking that we have reached a certain depth of healing and level in God that we very well may not have yet attained.

You must approach your inner healing journey with the full knowledge that it is a very "personal" one. Your inner healing journey is also one that will humble you.

I am always reminded of the scripture that tells us that we are not to think more highly of ourselves than we ought (Romans 12:3). As soon as we think we have made our "arrival" in life, we are always reminded that we constantly, consistently and desperately need God to make it through each and every moment.

Another equally important piece to the wholeness puzzle is the state and condition of your soul. 3 John 1:2 (KJV) says, Beloved, I wish above all things that thou mayest prosper and be in health, even as thy soul prospereth.

It is easy to celebrate your prosperity and the healthy areas in your life. Healthy areas in your life denote growth in a specific area. However, as you are progressing in these areas, it can be expected that your soul is just as healthy and nurtured.

Your soul is your mind, will and emotions. In other words, it's the fleshly part of you that connects you to the reality around you. Could it be that you aren't progressing as much as you think are because your soul is unhealthy?

Here are just a few things you can do if this is the case:

Renew your mind daily and train it to believe the word of God (Romans 12:1).

Reform your will until it is conformed into the will of God for you because Gods will is the safest (Luke 22:42).

Refine your emotions. Our traumas in life can cause our emotions to become unstable. Your emotions are inconsistent and don't deserve your trust. Refinement keeps your emotions pure (Philippians 4:6-7).

In summation, the progress of your life runs parallel with the state and condition of your soul. The best way to address your soul issues is to start in the presence of the Lord. There you can be free of condemnation, guilt and shame. You will never reach your full potential in God if you never address the issues that are housed in your soul. You must continually detox what is there. Your soul should be functioning healthily so that you can enjoy the life that God intended for you. More importantly, it is intended for you to live a life of wholeness as you pursue His plan and purpose for you.

First Forgive

Although your heart is now new (or becoming new) it is in need of constant and consistent care. Anything you leave unattended, neglected or anything that is void of prayer will begin to rely heavily on emotions, carnality and the past (including its victories) to survive. What you can't see futuristically you will take cues and lessons from the past and make up your now as you go. A clean and pure heart (Psalm 51:10) is essential. It is important that you develop a healthy spiritual regime immediately and check the contents of your heart daily (Psalm 139:23-24). Keep in mind that as you have now undergone a heart transplant and are taking on the nature and characteristics of the Father what you house in your heart will show up in your daily dealings. If it's not like God get rid of it immediately.

There are many things that war for our attention and as a result, get stored in our heart. One of the primary storage areas and key heart elements that will need your attention first is forgiveness. If you let webster define, what forgiveness is you may never ever experience the transformative power of Holy Spirit to give you the breakthrough that you need in this area. Forgiveness isn't optional for you to extend, forgiveness doesn't offer selections in specific areas we should forgive (or not) and forgiveness doesn't give the offender a pass, an endorsement or a license for how they mistreated you. What forgiveness does and longs to do is free you and clear the path to experience ALL Christ has for you. The circumstances of what caused the blockage don't excuse the conversations and discussions you will need to have (in the presence of the Lord) on finally letting it go.

It's time!

Take a look at this:

Mark 11:25 (**NLT)**

"But when you are praying, first forgive anyone you are holding a grudge against, so that your Father in heaven will forgive your sins, too."

So not only will the adversary try to get you *not to pray* and distract you from it but he will rob you by getting you to hold grudges and living a life that holds on to unforgiveness thus leaving YOUR sins on the line not to be forgiven.

If forgiveness is an area you struggle in allow me to suggest the following:

1. **Share** the details and the emotions attached to those details with God. Share with someone also that will hold you accountable.

2. **Shape** and frame at least 21 days to getting free from the offender (IN PRAYER) that hurt you. Yes! Even praying for them.

3. **See** your own sin. Yes, it hurt I know but we have also broke Gods heart and transgressed His law w our actions.

Lastly, you will have to repeat this as needed and as areas come up that you need to address regarding forgiveness. Forgiving QUICKLY is essential so that you don't waste years and years of your life bound to a person (dead or alive) a memory or hoping that through your own strength and might you will receive vindication. NO! Enter into your secret place and before you let God "have it" with request.... first forgive.

The Grace Not to Remain Bitter

Recently I encountered a challenge. Before the challenge, I had been seeing true change in my character and disposition especially in situations that attempted to steal my joy. I was slightly disappointed in myself to have given a reaction to this situation, but I also wanted more than ever to seek and attack the root. The day before my challenge I was driving, and the Lord began to deal with me about truth.

John 8:32 tells us that knowing the truth shall MAKE us free, so I believe we have to (know) and (embrace) truth FIRST in order to walk out real freedom. This task can be taxing. I asked myself does truth really hurt or is the making (the journey to freedom that truth promises us) more painful? I have read countless times in scripture where specific things are "made" and because in a moment we asked to be "made" we possibly limited God on what He wanted to make and accomplish in us. Lord make me "new", or "whole" or "over" when instead He just may simply be trying to "make what He wills". Trust Him enough that all He makes will be good including the internal work He's completing in you.

Where I am in my life truth is essential so receiving Holy Spirit's conversation on it was refreshing and overdue. However, this conversation didn't stop there because I discovered a truth about me that I otherwise may have denied: the root of bitterness. Yes, the "B" word. The discovery of a root (in you) can become an easy excuse. "It really wasn't that deep" "I am justified in what I feel" and "it's them and not me", regardless of it doesn't and most likely won't change what's present and what needs to be severed. I challenge you to do your own self-assessment on what may have attached itself to you (voluntarily or involuntarily). How can you tell if you're in need of an assessment? Through your frustrations, meditations and fluctuations.

Finally, I wanted to find a scripture that would help me see and hold me accountable. Upon my search I found:

Hebrews 12:15 English Standard Version (ESV)

15 See to it that no one fails to obtain the grace of God; that no "root of bitterness" springs up and causes trouble, and by it many become defiled.

I don't know about you but my fears, my preventative maintenance of a thing and my being exposed to others when it comes to my flaws has never guaranteed me not failing. Transparently speaking if I were to fail at anything I wouldn't want to fail at obtaining anything that would catapult me to deeper depths in God. Also, I wouldn't want to miss out on the grace of God. It's what has kept and enabled us to live a life of obedience in our walk and a life free of condemnation. Grace is the undeserved favor of God. So, when I saw this scripture, I first learned that what appears to be an unlimited supply of and an ocean filled with can dry up quickly and slip my grasp, how? If I don't deal with bitterness. If I don't lay my anger and my pain at the feet of Jesus. If I don't stop expecting repayment in some form for what "they" did and if I don't humble myself under Gods mighty hand.

Bitterness will cause trouble and defile us in other words it'll make you most like the one who's offended you.

As I close, I leave you with this, it is possible to frustrate and limit the grace of God afforded to us, but I just believe we can tap into "more Grace" that will combat what's attached to us and especially ask the Lord for more grace when dealing with the root of bitterness so that whatever you do you have this grace not to remain bitter.

Full blog catalog at: ambershonette.wordpress.com

REMEMBER

Thirst:

A key piece and area to ever being enough will come from your discipline and your identity. Until these are solidified you can decree all day how you are enough, but it will be futile. You have got to do what you don't feel like and then become. Becoming when the odds are against you and when you don't even look like who you know you are. If you start here, you will end well and finish strong. Have a healthy thirst and have a thirst that you know once you have mastered your discipline and identity you know God will quench every dry, desert like place in your life. The thirst is always real and authentic when you thirst for Him.

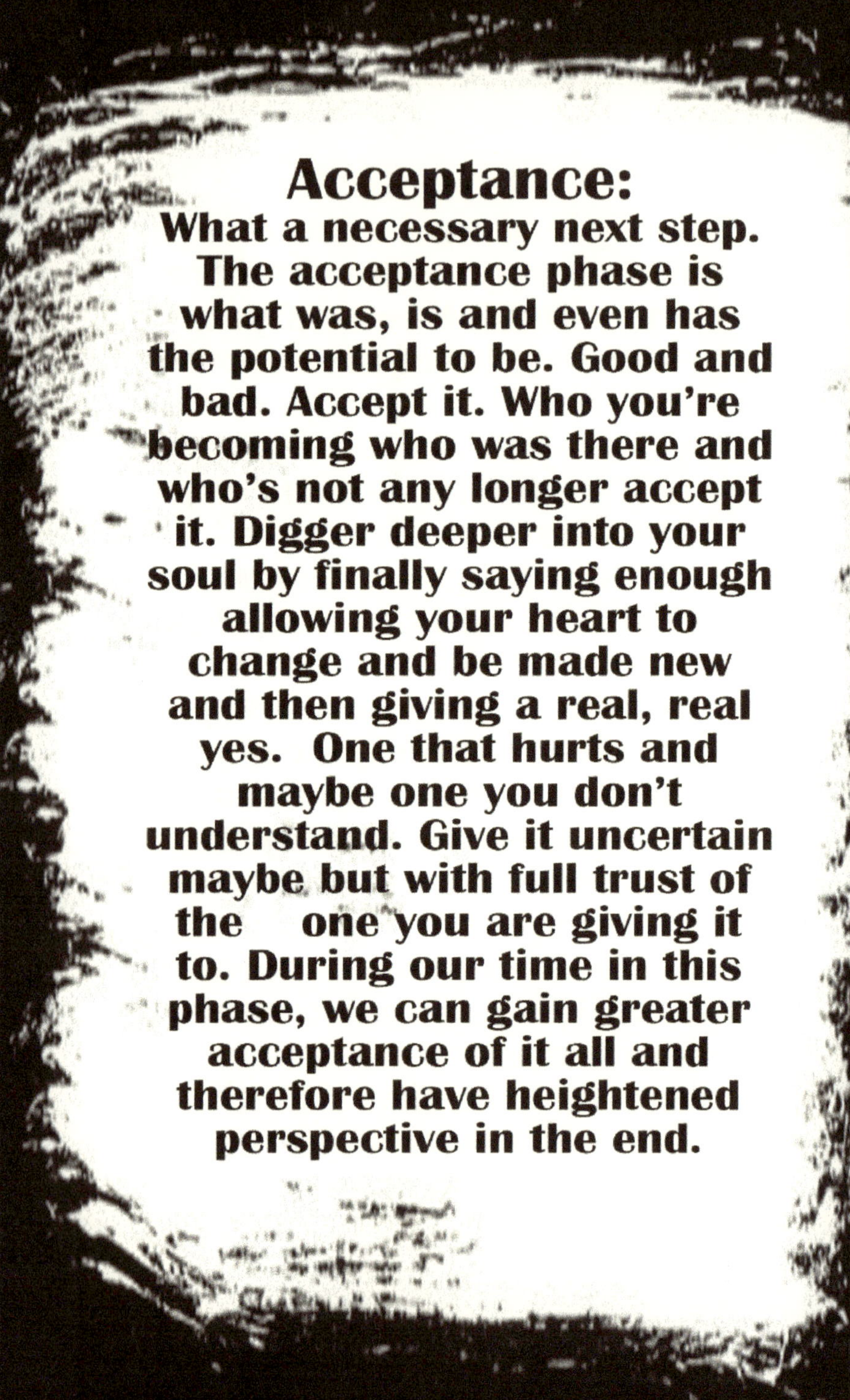
Acceptance:
What a necessary next step. The acceptance phase is what was, is and even has the potential to be. Good and bad. Accept it. Who you're becoming who was there and who's not any longer accept it. Digger deeper into your soul by finally saying enough allowing your heart to change and be made new and then giving a real, real yes. One that hurts and maybe one you don't understand. Give it uncertain maybe but with full trust of the one you are giving it to. During our time in this phase, we can gain greater acceptance of it all and therefore have heightened perspective in the end.

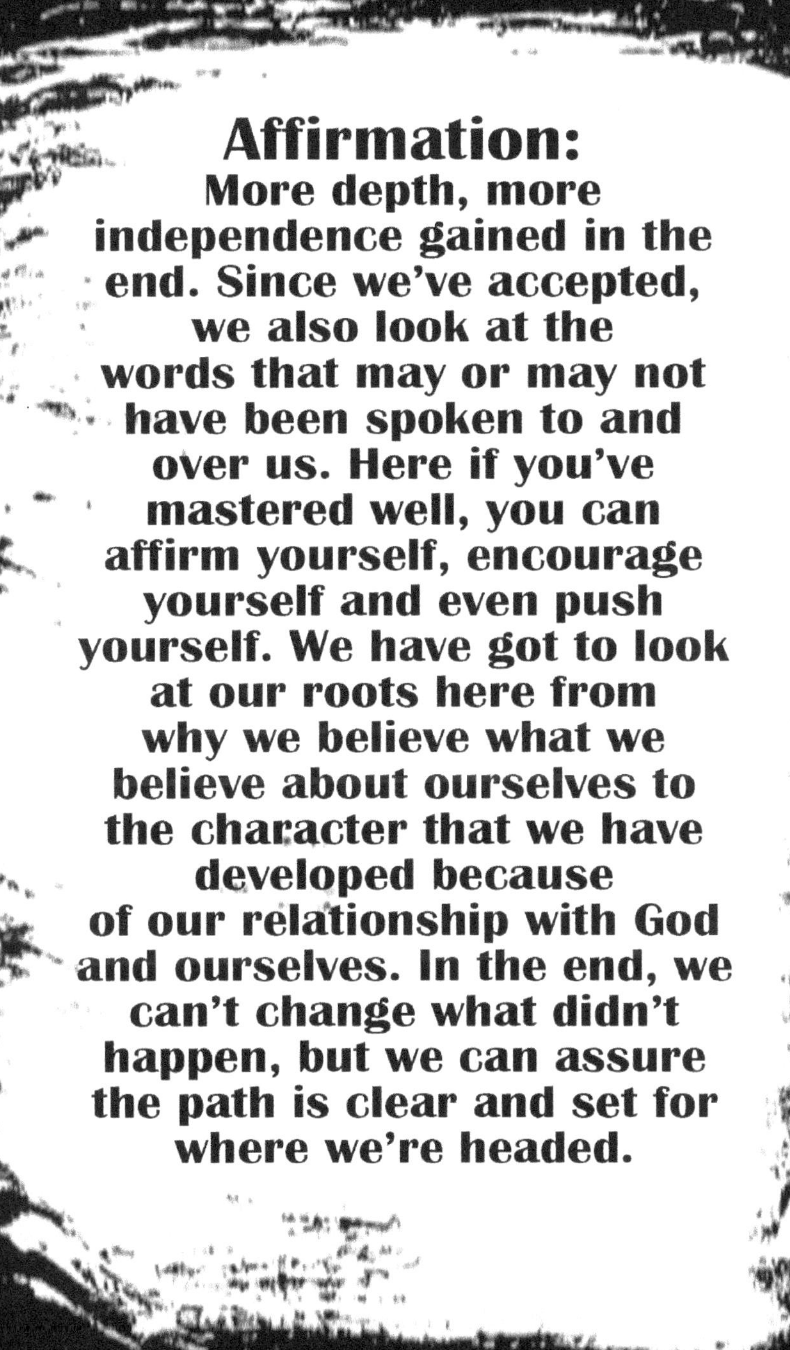

Affirmation:

More depth, more independence gained in the end. Since we've accepted, we also look at the words that may or may not have been spoken to and over us. Here if you've mastered well, you can affirm yourself, encourage yourself and even push yourself. We have got to look at our roots here from why we believe what we believe about ourselves to the character that we have developed because of our relationship with God and ourselves. In the end, we can't change what didn't happen, but we can assure the path is clear and set for where we're headed.

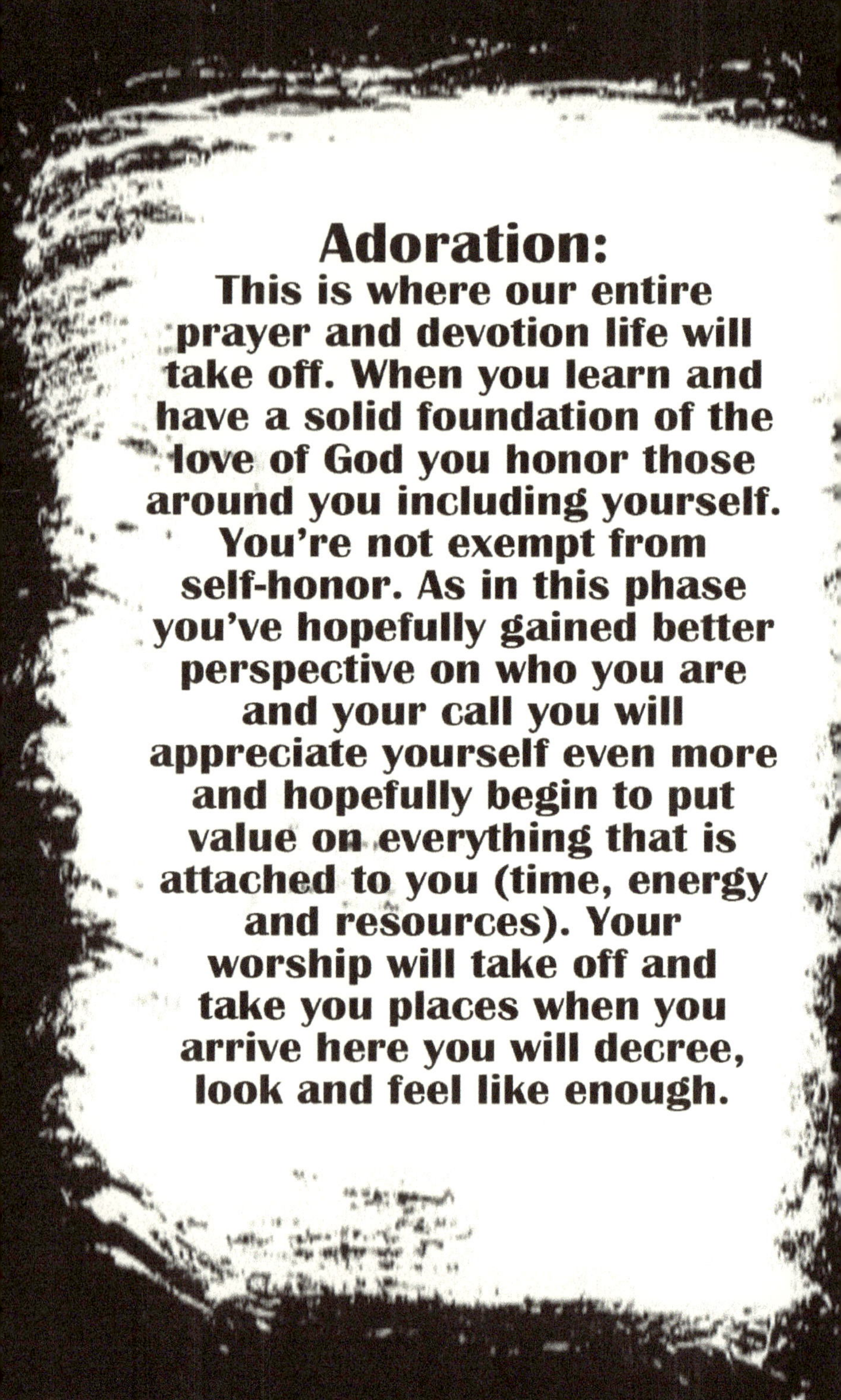

Adoration:

This is where our entire prayer and devotion life will take off. When you learn and have a solid foundation of the love of God you honor those around you including yourself. You're not exempt from self-honor. As in this phase you've hopefully gained better perspective on who you are and your call you will appreciate yourself even more and hopefully begin to put value on everything that is attached to you (time, energy and resources). Your worship will take off and take you places when you arrive here you will decree, look and feel like enough.

Confessions

Let's Confess!

Confession: noun a formal statement admitting that one is guilty of a crime.

One day I was discussing with my coach my desire to come from behind the pen and talk. Yes talk! There is power in your words and in your voice. Together we came up with confessions which is all about life, legacy and love too. But then as I was thinking heavily on impact and difference something else came as well. Much of what has stopped me and even stunted my growth was shared in this book and also wrapped up in one word: condemnation. So herein lies confessions.

No longer will we deny what we did (see definition above) but no longer will it also be what causes us to hide either. Confessions seeks to help others "crush condemnation". I started to learn the more I spoke that my nervousness was much, much deeper. I also started to learn the necessity for my voice and the impact I had and the stream that could be created through it as well. But even with all that knowledge I still would freeze, rely heavily on notes and have paralyzing fear. I want to talk to those that have been in this situation too and aren't sure how to overcome. You will be surprised at the level of revelation, healing and what can be broken off of you through a conversation.

So, a subsidiary of HerStory is Confessions where I and others will journey to break the back of condemnation in our stories and our minds. First admission, "I did it, but I am not it." I may have even said it in a moment of weakness and vulnerability but that too isn't the narrative of my story nor the narrative it will be based on. I am better than I was even yesterday, and fear will no longer paralyze, cripple and render me powerless. Details will be made available at ambershonette.com.

Afterword

I pray and hope that our time together and all that I have shared has been beneficial. I pray that you close this book leaving strengthened and encouraged about who you are. I pray that you see the value in every obstacle that you have managed to overcome. I pray going forward you see nothing but victory.

Being enough is more than a mantra and a bold statement but it starts within. I chose to write this book because I know all too well the affects that rejection can cause. It's tough and hard (rejection). Yes, it was for your protection but also for your redirection. Things happened in certain ways to re direct or reroute you back on track. Writing this book caused me to reflect on moments where I longed for people to stay and almost didn't make room for those that desired to be present. Writing this book caused me to reflect on my value being named and placed in the hands of the highest bidder instead of being sought and solidified in the presence of a merciful savior.

I am so grateful and thankful for the strength and the courage once again to do this. This is what I was born for, and I am also thankful that I have leaped over yet another hurdle in my journey. Her Story was started because I needed an outlet and a haven to be able to not succumb to trauma and tribulation. I needed to make sense of all I have faced and why God not only chose me but deals with me the way He does.

From now until we will no longer take moments like these for granted. We will no longer let seasons stick around longer than they came to be with us, and we won't diminish who we are by who's not with us. Instead, we will rise high, we will flourish, and, in our disappointments, we will know that better is near the sooner we let go.
We will fight on our knees extend the utmost mercy and grace and we will without a doubt decree through it all "I Am Enough".

~Amber Shonette

About the Author

Amber Shonette Burwell is a mother, grandmother, teacher, certified coach and author, more importantly a lover of and loved by God. Born in Brooklyn N.Y and raised in Queens N.Y Amber relocated to Virginia Beach in the late 90's. It wasn't until 2013 that Amber picked up one of her first loves (writing) again under the banner of and by way of HerStory.

As the founder of HerStory the mission is to assist those that have had traumatic experiences, deep wounds and simply stuck in the past to live in purpose in spite of opposition, to stir their gifts all while focusing on Christ.

In 2014 Amber would publish her first book and autobiography A Glimpse of Her Story Vol. I at the same time becoming a professional blogger. After this Amber would go on to assist several authors on their own self-publishing journey.
In 2021 Amber would go on to publish again this time Vol. II of A Glimpse of HerStory entitled "I Am Enough" a book to empower both men and women in their identity and in their soul.

With other projects in the works such as confessions, dear beautiful soul and Big Ma's house under the banner of HerStory it's important to Amber that those entrusted to her *release regret and crush condemnation*. Later this year Amber will release her highly anticipated podcast.

Amber resides in Virginia Beach, Virginia, is a full-time healthcare recruiter and in pursuit of a Bachelor of Science degree in Communication at Walden University.

www.ingramcontent.com/pod-product-compliance
Lightning Source LLC
Chambersburg PA
CBHW030830090426
42737CB00009B/945

9780578852010